MY VERY FIRST

Number Book

ANGELA WILKES

D1088640

[DK]

A DK PUBLISHING BOOK

www.dk.com

First American Edition, 1993
8 10 9

Published in the United States by
DK Publishing, Inc., 375 Hudson Street,
New York, New York 10014

Copyright © 1993 Dorling Kindersley Limited, London

Photography (p.11 fish; p.15 ladybug)
copyright © 1991 Jerry Young

ISBN 1-56458-376-7

Color reproduction by Colourscan
Printed and bound in Italy by L.E.G.O.

Contents

Note to parents and teachers

My Very First Number Book is a bright and colorful book for you and your child to share. Packed with photographs of everyday objects, it is the ideal way to introduce young children to numbers and counting.

Your child will benefit most from the book if you work through it together. You can practice counting up to twenty and explore early number concepts, such as matching, sorting, and adding.

It is important for children to take time with each step. **My Very First Number Book** is designed to allow children to fully grasp one concept before moving on to the next. But the most important aspect of early number learning is enjoyment. The wealth of colorful objects and simple puzzles will capture your child's attention and help make numbers enticing and fun.

With so many pictures to look at and talk about, this book offers a wide range of other learning opportunities. You can encourage your child to identify and name the objects on the page and in the world around them, and introduce concepts such as shapes, sizes, colors, and patterns.

Counting up

Can you count from one to ten?

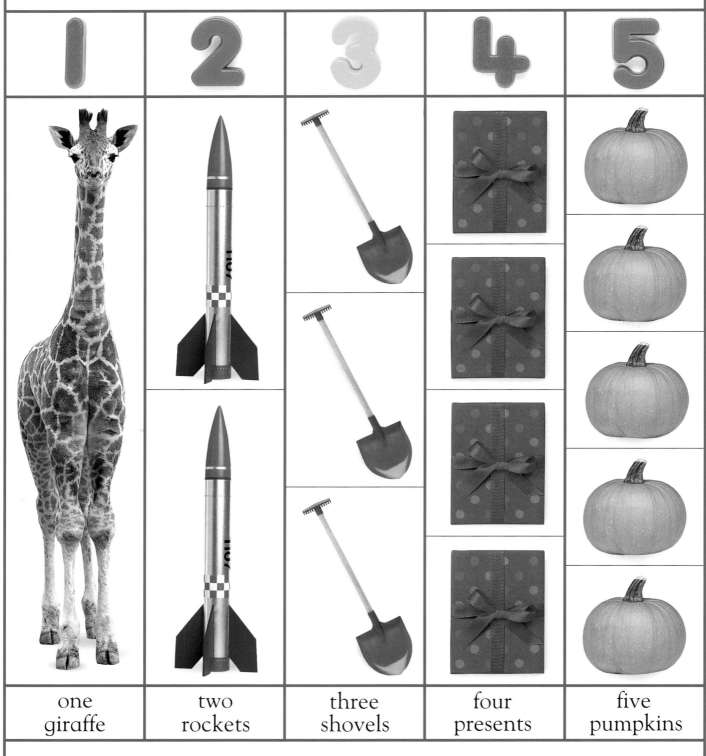

1	2	3	4	5
one giraffe	two rockets	three shovels	four presents	five pumpkins

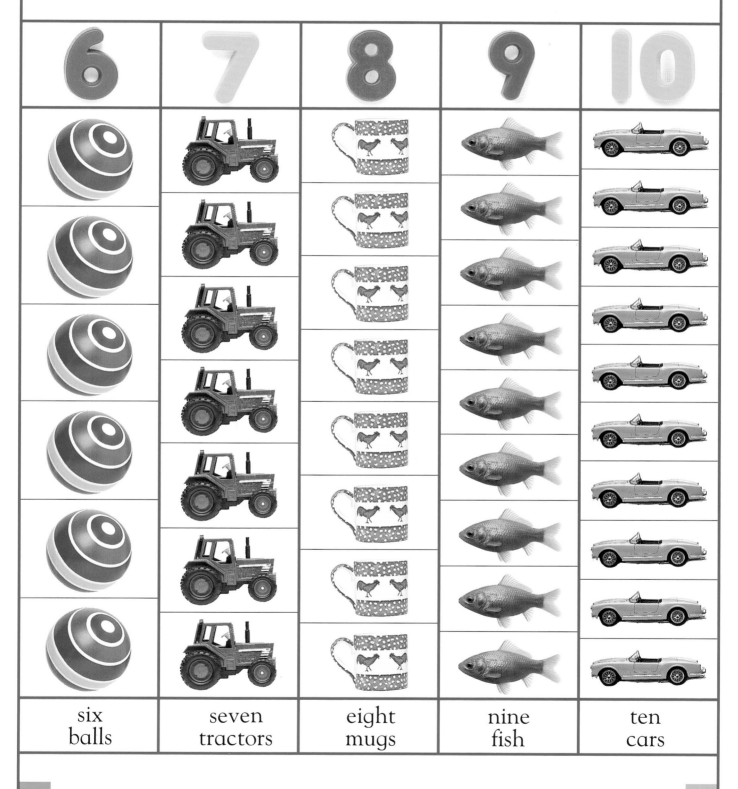

6	7	8	9	10
six balls	seven tractors	eight mugs	nine fish	ten cars

Counting to twenty

Can you count to twenty?

11	12	13	14	15
eleven toy cars	twelve snails	thirteen sunglasses	fourteen buttons	fifteen forks

16	17	18	19	20
sixteen marbles	seventeen sharpeners	eighteen umbrellas	nineteen shells	twenty pencils

How many?

Snails and frogs

How many toy snails
do you count?

How many toy frogs
do you count?

Party time!

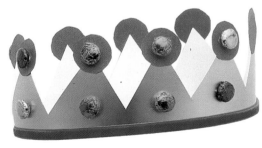

How many party
blowers do
you count?

How many party hats
do you count?

Counting colors

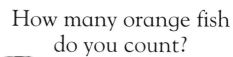

How many orange fish
do you count?

How many blue fish
are swimming by?

How many fish
in all?

Counting shapes

How many squares
do you count?

How many circles
do you count?

Are they the same?

Toy train

How many blocks in this pile?
Are there as many blocks in
the train car as in the pile?

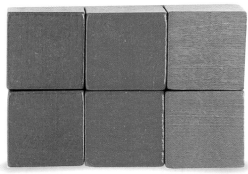

Fruit bowl

How many bananas in the bowl?
Is the number of bananas
not in the bowl
the same?

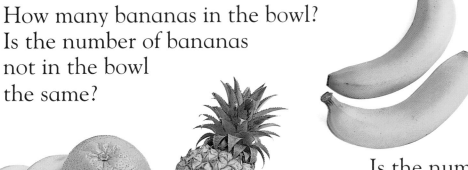

Is the number of pineapples
in the bowl the same as the
number not in the bowl?

Are there as many strawberries
not in the bowl as there
are in the bowl?

Children

Count the children in each of these groups. Is the number of children in each group the same?

Peas in a pod

Is the number of peas inside the pod the same as the number outside?

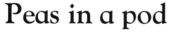

Puppies

Is the number of puppies in each group the same?

More or less?

Oranges and lemons

Count the fruit on each plate.

Which plate has more fruit?

Buttons

How many buttons
do you count?

Are there more square buttons
than round buttons?

Snakes

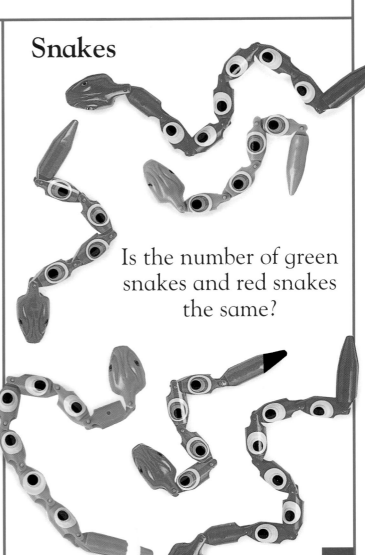

Is the number of green
snakes and red snakes
the same?

14

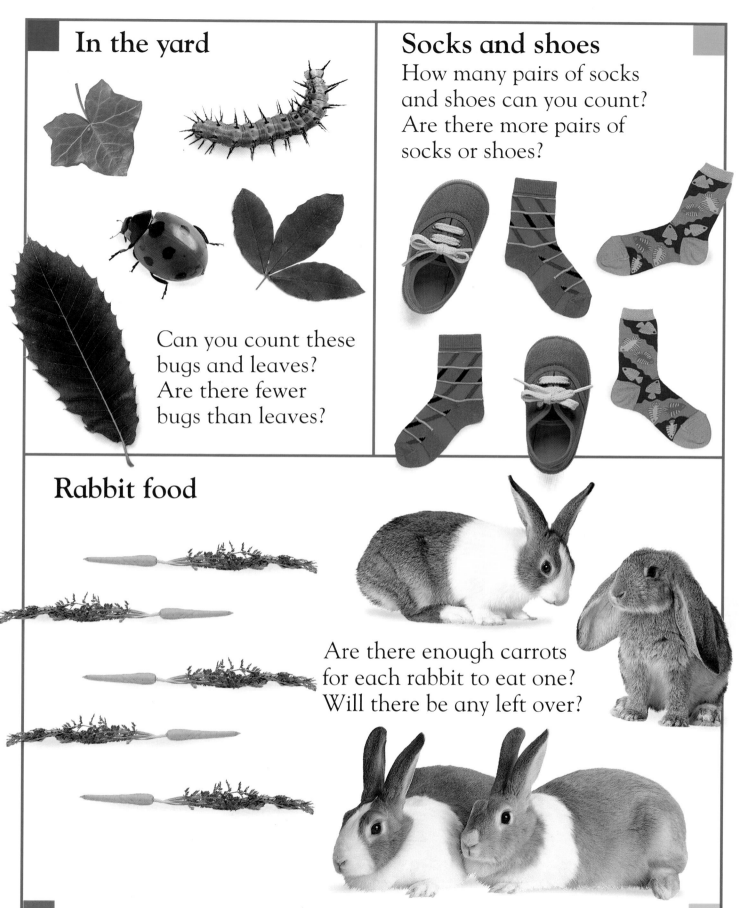

In the yard

Can you count these bugs and leaves? Are there fewer bugs than leaves?

Socks and shoes

How many pairs of socks and shoes can you count? Are there more pairs of socks or shoes?

Rabbit food

Are there enough carrots for each rabbit to eat one? Will there be any left over?

Matching numbers

Sort the animals into groups. How many in each group?
Can you find a matching number below?

Garden puzzle

Can you count the objects on the tiles and find a number to match? When you find a matching pair, cover them with coins.

Here is an example to help you.

Find the number

Numbers are all around us. Have you seen any of these everyday objects with numbers on them?

Can you use a calculator?

Can you tell the times on this clock and watch?

Do you know your telephone number?

What does the number on this box tell us?

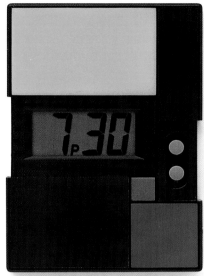

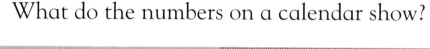

This clock shows the time with digital numbers.

What do the numbers on a calendar show?

What does this price tag tell us?

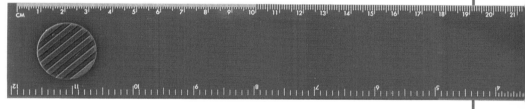

We use a ruler to measure length.

Why do we use a measuring pitcher?

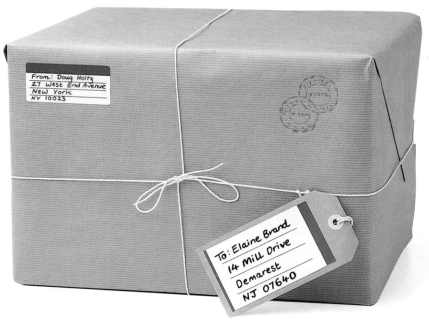

Why are there numbers on this label?

How many in all?

We add things to find out how many there are in all.

Butterfly flight

2 pretty butterflies   2 more are added   How many in all?

Puppet show

3 funny finger puppets   1 more is added   How many in all?

Bunches of flowers

4 colorful flowers   2 more are added   How many in all?

More number questions

We can use numbers and symbols to write number questions.

This symbol means "add."

This symbol means "how many in all?"

Can you work out the answers to these number questions?

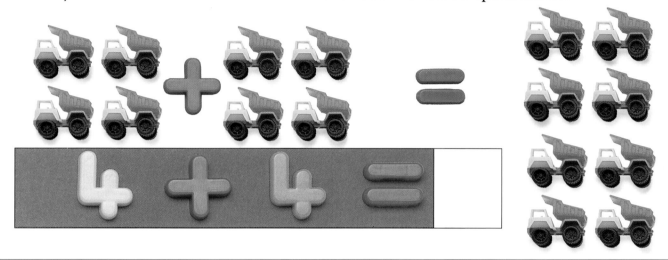

4 + 4 =

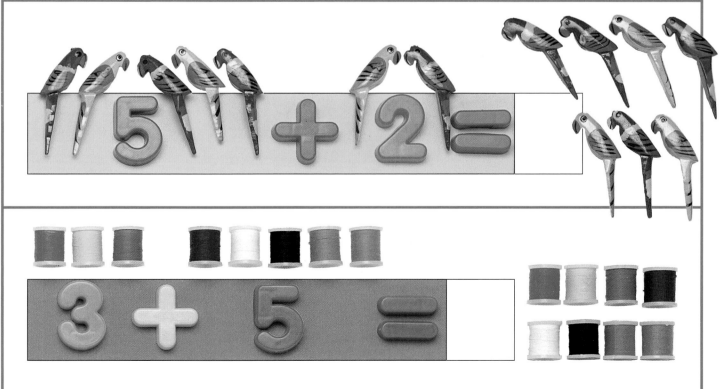

5 + 2 =

3 + 5 =